Better Drums With...
Rockschool

www.rockschool.co.uk

Welcome To Drums Grade 5

Welcome to the Rockschool Drums Grade 8 pack. The book and CD contain everything needed to play drums in this grade. In the book you will find the exam scores in drums notation. The accompanying CD has full stereo mixes of each tune, backing tracks to play along with for practice, one with a click and one without for each song, and spoken two bar count-ins to each piece. Handy tips on playing the pieces and the marking schemes can be found in the Guru's Guide on page 22. If you have any queries about this or any other Rockschool exam, please call us on **020 8332 6303**, email us at *info@rockschool.co.uk* or visit our website *www.rockschool.co.uk*. Good luck!

Level 2 Requirements for Grades 4 & 5

The nine Rockschool grades are divided into four levels. These levels correspond to the levels of the National Qualifications Framework (NQF). Further details about the NQF can be found at *www.qca.org.uk/NQF*. Details of all Rockschool's accredited qualifications can be found at *www.qca.org.uk/openquals*.

Drums Grade 5 is part of Level 2. This Level is for those of you who are confident in all the key basic skills on drums and who are stepping up to more advanced skills and stylistic expression.

Grade 4: in this grade you will use a range of physical and expressive techniques with confidence including those drawn from the technical exercise section of the exam. The rhythms are more complex with sixteenth and dotted notes and the syncopations are now also more complex. You will be experimenting with a range of dynamics from very quiet (*pp*) to very loud (*ff*). It is at this grade that you are continuing to develop your ability to play with stylistic sensitivity and authority.

Grade 5: as a player you will be confident in a range of physical and expressive techniques. You will be able to demonstrate your abilities across a number of styles and have control over sound and volume adjustments to suit the playing styles of your choice.

Drums Exams at Grade 5

There are **three** types of exam that can be taken using this pack: a Grade Exam, a Performance Certificate and a Band Exam.

Drums Grade 5 Exam: this is for players who want to develop performance and technical skills

Players wishing to enter for a Drums Grade 5 exam need to prepare **three** pieces of which **one** may be a free choice piece chosen from outside the printed repertoire. In addition you must prepare the technical exercises in the book, undertake either a sight reading test or an improvisation & interpretation test, take an ear test and answer general musicianship questions. Samples of these tests are printed in the book along with audio examples on the CD.

Drums Grade 5 Performance Certificate: this is for players who want to focus on performing in a range of styles

To enter for your Drums Grade 5 Performance Certificate you play pieces only. You can choose any **five** of the six tunes printed in this book, or you can choose to bring in up to **two** free choice pieces as long as they meet the standards set out by Rockschool. Free choice piece checklists for all grades can be found on the Rockschool website: *www.rockschool.co.uk*.

Level 2 Band Exam in Guitar, Bass and Drums: this is for players who want to play in a band

The Level 2 band exam is for all of you who would like to play the repertoire at Grade 5 as a three piece band, consisting of guitar, bass and drums. You play together in the exam, using the parts printed in the Grade 5 Guitar, Bass and Drum books. Like the Drums Grade 5 Performance Certificate, you play any **five** of the six printed tunes, or you can include up to **two** free choice pieces as long as they meet the standards set out by Rockschool. If you take this exam you will be marked as a unit with each player expected to contribute equally to the overall performance of each piece played.

Drums Notation Explained

DRUM VOICES
The drums are arranged
around the staff as follows.

1. Kick drum	6. Buzz Snare	11. Hi hat closed
2. Floor tom	7. Medium tom	12. Hi hat open *
3. Snare drum	8. High tom	13. Crash cymbal *
4. Rim shot	9. Ride cymbal *	14. Hi hat (foot)
5. Ghost snare	10. Ride cymbal on bell *	15. Hi hat open (foot) *
		16. Hi hat (foot) and kick drum together

* For clarity, all cymbals,
regardless of rhythmic value,
ring on unless specifically
marked as choked.

General Musical Notation

(accent) • Accentuate note (play it louder).

Fill

• Ad lib. section played around the
kit, often at the end of a section.

(accent) • Accentuate note with great intensity.

• Repeat bars between signs.

Choke

• After striking either the crash
or the ride cymbal, grasp the
cymbal rim to prevent it from
ringing on.

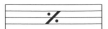

1.   2.

• When a repeated section has
different endings, play the first
ending only the first time and
the second ending only the
second time.

D.%. al Coda

• Go back to the sign (%), then play until
the bar marked *To Coda* ⊕ then skip to
the section marked ⊕ *Coda*.

• Repeat previous bar. In higher
grades these may also be marked
sim. or *cont. sim.*

D.C. al Fine

• Go back to the beginning of the song and
play until the bar marked *Fine* (end).

2

• Repeat previous 2 bars. In higher
grades these may also be marked
sim. or *cont. sim.*

Alka Setzer

Simon Troup

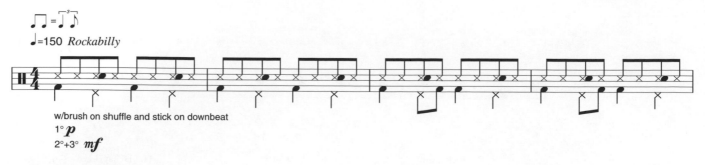

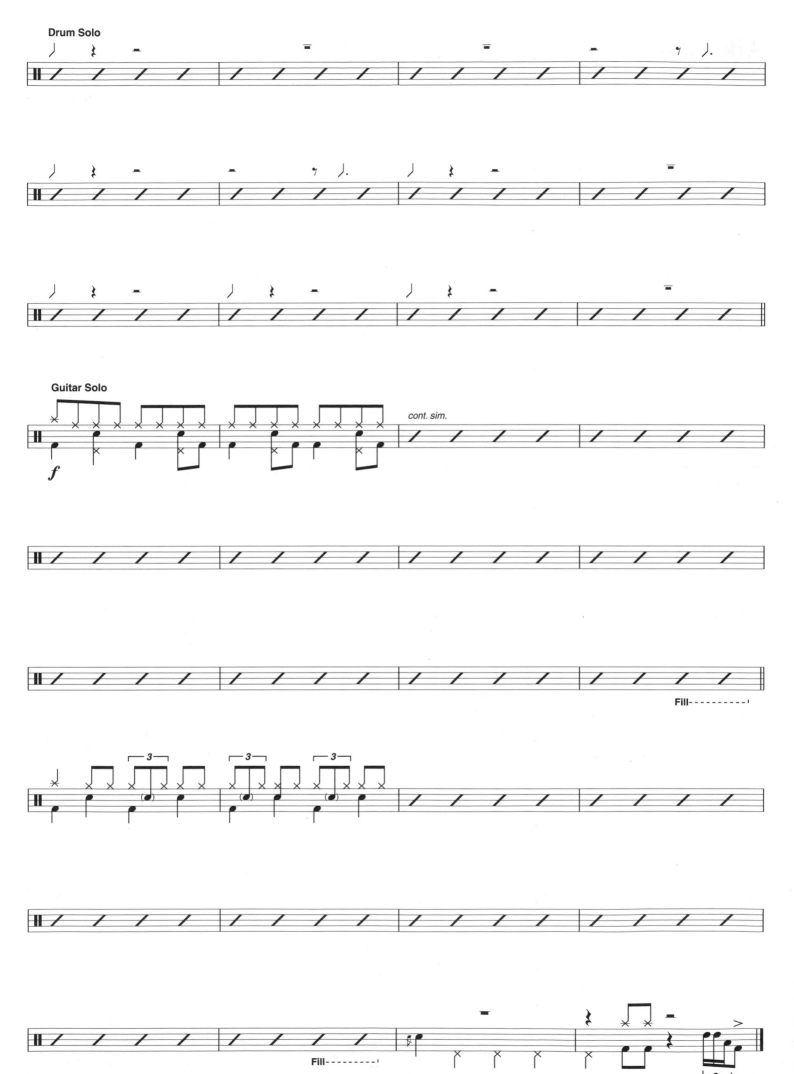

Sidewinder

Tracks 2, 8 & 14

Hussein Boon

To Coda ⊕

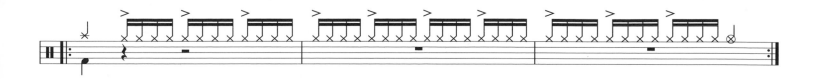

Fill

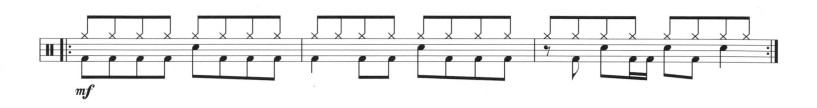

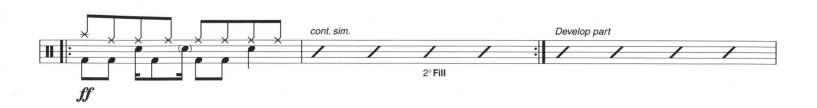

Develop part

2° Fill

D.%. al Coda ⊕
No repeats

⊕ Coda

© 2006 Rock School Ltd.

This music is copyright. Photocopying is illegal.

All Funked Up

Jason Woolley

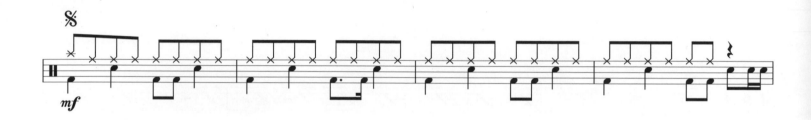

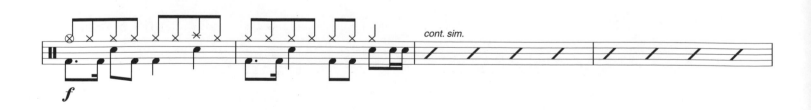

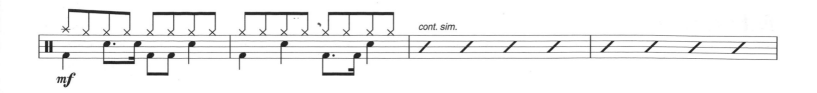

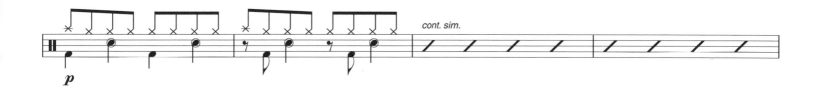

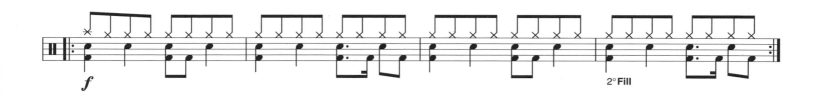

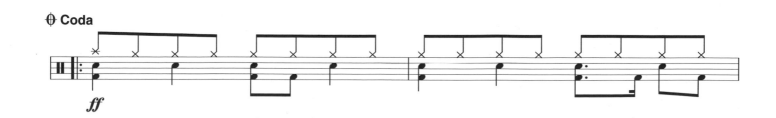

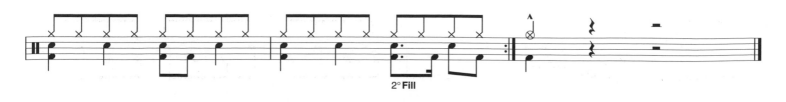

D & A

Noam Lederman

♩=120 *Britpop*
w/ad lib. cymbals & toms

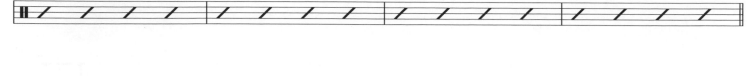

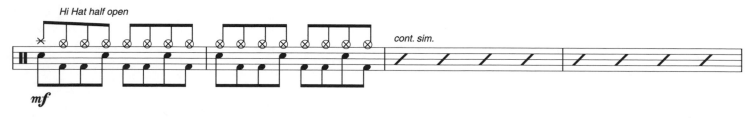

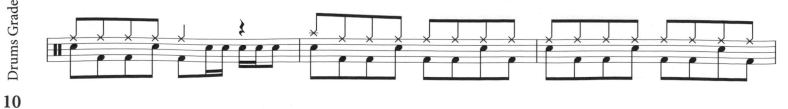

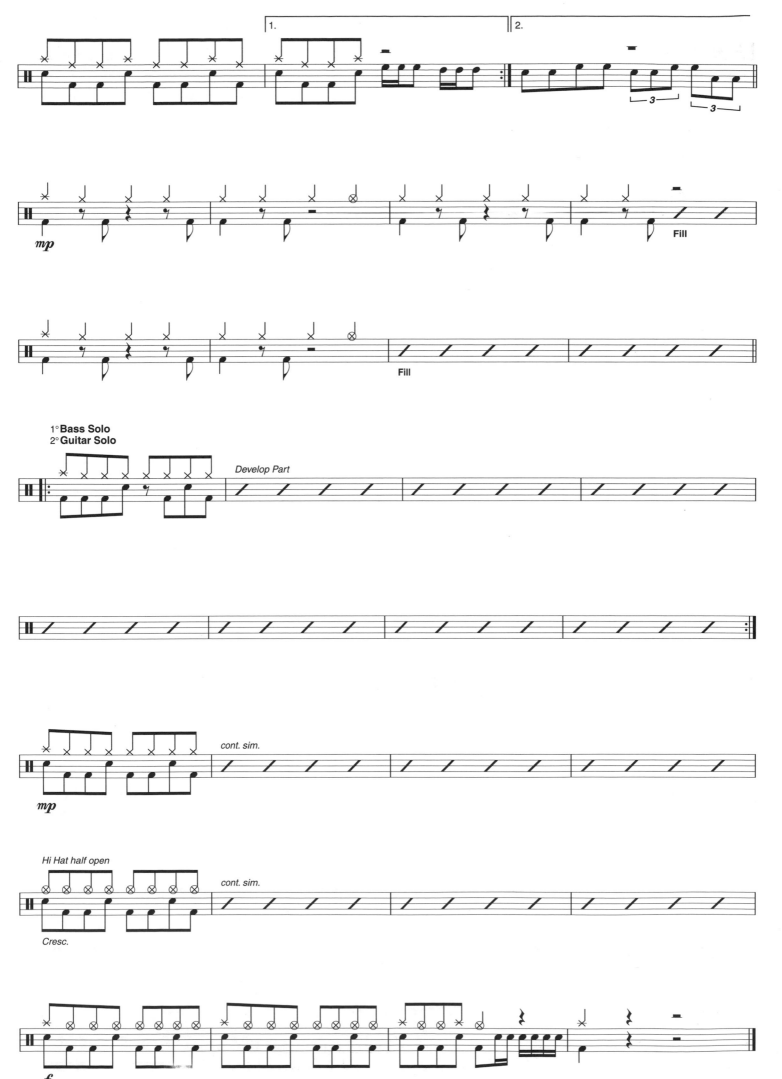

Bust Up

Joe Bennett & Simon Troup

Drums Grade 5

Grade Exam and Performance Certificate Entry Form

Please complete the form below in BLOCK CAPITALS. Information given below will only be used by Rockschool for exam purposes and for Rockschool news. Completed application forms should be sent, along with a cheque made payable to '**Rockschool**' for the appropriate fees, to:

Exam Entries, Rockschool, Evergreen House, 2-4 King Street, Twickenham, Middlesex, TW1 3RZ

---

1. Candidate's Details

Full Name (as it will appear on the certificate):

Date of Birth (DD/MM/YY)*:　　　　Gender (M/F)*:　　　*This information is compulsory but will be used for statistical purposes only

Address:

　　　　　　　　　　　　　　　　　　　　　Postcode:

Telephone No:　　　　　　　　　　　　Mobile No:

Email address:

☐ (Please tick) **Yes!** I would like to receive all correspondence from Rockschool via email (with the exception of certificates and mark sheets which will be posted). *Rockschool will NOT circulate your email address to any third parties.*

---

2. Your Examination

Type of Exam (Grade or Performance Certificate):　　　　　　Grade:

Instrument:　　　　　　　*If you are applying for multiple examinations, please continue below:*

| Type of Exam: | Instrument: | Grade: |
| Type of Exam: | Instrument: | Grade: |

Period (A/B/C)*:　　　　　*Refer to our website for exam periods and closing dates*

Preferred Town for Examination (*Refer to our website for a list of current towns with Rockschool examination centres*):

Rockschool will endeavour to place you at your preferred town, but cannot guarantee this

Please state any dates that are IMPOSSIBLE for you to attend*:

It is not guaranteed that we can avoid these dates

---

3. Additional information

Drum Candidates. Do you require a left-handed kit?

Will you be bringing your own kit (Grades 6,7,8 only)?　　　　If 'no' Rockschool will provide a drum kit.

Popular Piano Candidates. Will you be bringing your own keyboard?

If 'no', Rockschool can provide either a keyboard or a piano. Please indicate which you prefer :

Special Needs Candidates. Please include a supporting letter with your application explaining your requirements.

All Candidates. If there is any additional information you consider relevant, please attach a note to your application.

---

4. Fees — *For current exam prices please refer to our website, www.rockschool.co.uk or call us on 0845 460 4747*

Fee enclosed:

Cheque Number:　　　　　　　　　　　　　PLEASE WRITE CANDIDATE NAME ON BACK OF CHEQUE

ROCKSCHOOL HELPLINE: 0845 460 4747
email: info@rockschool.co.uk　website: www.rockschool.co.uk

Teacher's Exam Entry Form

Teachers wishing to enter **grade exams** and **performance certificates** on behalf of their students should complete the form below in BLOCK CAPITALS. Information given will only be used by Rockschool for exam purposes and for Rockschool news. You can get up to date information on examination prices from **www.rockschool.co.uk** or by ringing the Rockschool helpline on **0845 460 4747**. Completed application forms should be sent, along with a cheque made payable to '**Rockschool**' for the appropriate fees, to:

Exam Entries, Rockschool, Evergreen House, 2-4 King Street, Twickenham, Middlesex, TW1 3RZ

1. Teacher's Details
Title (Mr/Mrs/Ms etc): Full Name:
Address:
Postcode:
Telephone No: Mobile No:
Email address:
For school entries please include your NCN (National Centre Number):
☐ (Please tick) **Yes!** I would like to receive all correspondence from Rockschool via email (with the exception of certificates and mark sheets which will be posted). *Rockschool will NOT circulate your email address to any third parties.*

2. Examination Details and Fees *For grade exams, please write 'G' and the grade number in the Grade box (e.g. **G6** for Grade 6). For performance certificates, please write '**PC**' and the grade number in the Grade box (e.g. **PC4** for Performance Certificate Grade 4). †For examination periods refer to our website. Continue on separate sheet if necessary.*
FOR SPECIAL NEEDS CANDIDATES PLEASE ATTACH A SUPPORTING LETTER WITH DETAILS.

Candidate's Name (as it will appear on the certificate)	Date of Birth	Gender (M/F)	Instrument	Grade*	Period†	Fee (£)
1.	DD MM YYYY					
2.	DD MM YYYY					
3.	DD MM YYYY					
4.	DD MM YYYY					
5.	DD MM YYYY					
6.	DD MM YYYY					
7.	DD MM YYYY					
8.	DD MM YYYY					
9.	DD MM YYYY					
10.	DD MM YYYY					
11.	DD MM YYYY					
12.	DD MM YYYY					
					Total fees enclosed £	

Preferred Town for Examination (*Refer to our website for a list of current towns with Rockschool examination centres*):

*Rockschool will endeavour to place your candidates at your preferred town, but cannot guarantee this

Please list dates your candidate(s) **cannot** attend*:

*It is not guaranteed that we can avoid these dates

Band Exam Entry Form

You can enter for one of the following band exams (1 Guitar player, 1 Bass player, 1 Drummer) using Rockschool materials: *Level One (Grade 3 repertoire)* * Level Two (Grade 5 repertoire) *Level Three (Grade 8 repertoire)*
Please complete the form below in BLOCK CAPITALS. Information given will only be used by Rockschool for exam purposes and for Rockschool news. Completed application forms should be sent, along with a cheque made payable to 'Rockschool' for the appropriate fees, to:

Exam Entries, Rockschool, Evergreen House, 2-4 King Street, Twickenham, Middlesex, TW1 3RZ

1. Band's Details
GUITARIST Full Name (as it will appear on the certificate):
Date of Birth (DD/MM/YY)*:   Gender (M/F)*:
BASSIST Full Name (as it will appear on the certificate):
Date of Birth (DD/MM/YY)*:   Gender (M/F)*:
DRUMMER Full Name (as it will appear on the certificate):
Date of Birth (DD/MM/YY)*:   Gender (M/F)*:
*This information is compulsory but will be used for statistical purposes only

2. Band's Main Contact Details
Main Contact's Name:
Address:
Postcode:
Telephone No: Mobile No:
Email address:
☐ (Please tick) **Yes!** I would like to receive all correspondence from Rockschool via email (with the exception of certificates and mark sheets which will be posted). *Rockschool will NOT circulate your email address to any third parties.*

3. Your Examination — *If you are applying for multiple exams, please use a separate form for each*
Exam Level (One/Two/Three):
Period (A/B/C)*:   *Refer to our website for exam periods and closing dates*
Preferred Town for Examination (*Refer to our website for a list of current towns with Rockschool examination centres**):
*Rockschool will endeavour to place you at your preferred town, but cannot guarantee this
Please state any dates that are IMPOSSIBLE for you to attend*:
*It is not guaranteed that we can avoid these dates
Additional Information *If there is any additional information you consider relevant (e.g. band members with special needs) please attach a separate sheet explaining your requirements.*

4. Fees — *For current exam prices please refer to our website, www.rockschool.co.uk or call us on 0845 460 4747*
Fee enclosed:
Cheque Number: PLEASE WRITE CANDIDATES' NAMES ON BACK OF CHEQUE

ROCKSCHOOL HELPLINE: 0845 460 4747
email: info@rockschool.co.uk   website: www.rockschool.co.uk

ROCKSCHOOL RESOURCES

At Rockschool we recognise the importance of keeping teachers and learners up to date with developments. Below are listed the qualifications and resources on offer. If you have any questions, please contact us through the relevant email address, or phone us on **0845 460 4747**.

PERFORMANCE DIPLOMAS

Music Performance Diploma
(DipRSL Perf) at Level 4

Music Performance Licentiate
(LRSL Perf) at Level 6

The Rockschool Performance Diplomas provide flexible, vocationally relevant qualifications for experienced or skilled performers of popular music.

diplomas@rockschool.co.uk

TEACHING DIPLOMAS

Teaching Diploma
(DipRSL) at Level 4
Teaching Diploma
(LRSL) at Level 6

The Rockschool Teaching Diplomas have been devised for instrumentalists, vocalists and music technologists who would like to attain a teaching qualification without having to attend a course or write essays. The diplomas focus on the practicalities of teaching and are neither genre nor instrument specific.

diplomas@rockschool.co.uk

MUSIC PRACTITIONERS QUALIFICATIONS

Rockschool/ATM
14-19 Diploma
Compatible

These flexible, vocationally relevant popular music qualifications will provide learners with the necessary skills to develop realistic employment opportunities in the music industry.

qualifications@rockschool.co.uk

COMPANION GUIDES

Sight Reading (Grades 1-8)
Improvisation & Interpretation
(Grades 1-5)
QSPs (Grades 6-8)
Ear Tests (Grades 1-8)
GMQs (Grades 1-8)

A must for any music teacher or self-taught musician using the Rockschool grade system. Rockschool Companion Guides contain examples of the exercises you will encounter in an exam along with tips on how best to perform.

info@rockschool.co.uk

Companion Guides available for purchase through **www.musicroom.com**

GUITAR DVDS

Following DVDs available:
Grades Debut & 1
Grade 2
Grade 3

Perfect for anyone working through the Rockschool grades, Rockschool DVDs include instructional lessons on how to make the most of the pieces and technical exercises required in your exams.

info@rockschool.co.uk

DVDs available for purchase through **www.musicroom.com**

COMING SOON...REPERTOIRE BOOKS

Rockschool Repertoire Books contain popular songs from rock through to indie. **Drums Grades 1 to 3** will be available from October 2008.

info@rockschool.co.uk

Repertoire Books soon available for purchase through **www.musicroom.com**

X-Blues III

Deirdre Cartwright

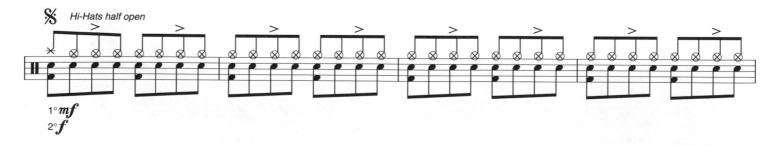

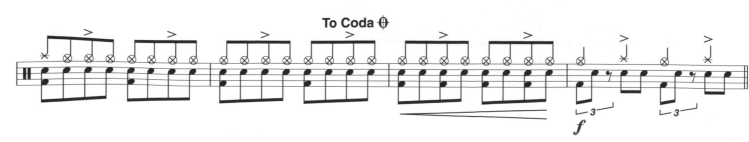

Guitar Solo

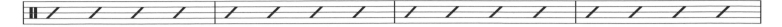

Bass Solo

D.%. al Coda

Coda

Technical Exercises

In this section, the examiner will ask you to play a selection of exercises drawn from each of the five groups shown below. In addition there is a fill exercise which you will play using the designated backing track on the CD. You do not need to memorise the exercises (and can use your book in the exam) but the examiner will be looking for the speed of your response. The examiner will also give credit for the level of your musicality.

The stickings shown (L & R) are there as a guide for right handed drummers. Left handed drummers should reverse the sticking patterns. **All exercises must be played to a metronome click.**

Group A: Single & Double Strokes ♩=80

You will be asked to play this as a continuous sequence in either single or double strokes by the examiner

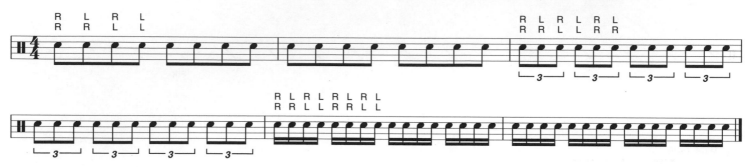

Group B: Paradiddles ♩=80

1. Standard paradiddle in sixteenth notes using snare and hi hat (kick drum follows hi hat)

2. Inverted paradiddle in sixteenth notes using snare and hi hat (kick drum follows hi hat)

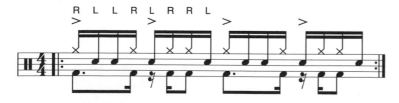

Group C: Rolls ♩=75

1. Five stroke roll

2. Seven stroke roll

Group D: Flams, Drags & Ruffs ♩=80

1. Flams in triplet eighth notes

2. Drag Tap

3. Ruffs in quarter notes

Group E: Hands & and Feet Patterns ♩=90

1. Pattern 1

2. Pattern 2

3. Pattern 3

4. Pattern 4

Group F: Fill

In the exam you will be asked to play the three bar groove shown below followed by the second bar of one of the Hands & Feet patterns (A–D) shown in Group E above chosen by the examiner. You will perform this exercise in the exam to the CD backing track.

♩=90 *Metal*

Sight Reading

In this section you have a choice between **either** a sight reading test **or** an improvisation & interpretation test (see facing page). Printed below is the type of sight reading test you are likely to encounter in the exam. At this level there is also an element of improvisation. This is in the form of a two bar drum fill. This piece will be composed in the style of blues, rock, funk or jazz and will be twelve bars long and may contain repeats. The examiner will allow you 90 seconds to prepare it and will set the tempo for you on a metronome. The tempo is ♩=90.

Improvisation & Interpretation

Printed below is an example of the type of improvisation & interpretation test you are likely to encounter in an exam. At this level there is a small element of sight reading. This takes the form of a two bar groove at the beginning of the test. You will be asked to play the groove and continue an improvised line to a backing track lasting twelve bars in the style of blues, rock, funk or jazz played by the examiner on CD. You will be allowed 30 seconds to prepare. You will then be allowed to practise through one playing of the test on the CD before playing it a second time for the exam. This test is continuous with a one bar count in at the beginning and after the practice session. The tempo is ♩ = 100.

Ear Tests

There are two ear tests in this grade. The examiner will play each test to you on CD. You will find one example of each type of test you will be given in the exam printed below.

Test 1: Fill Recognition

The examiner will play you one bar of snare drum fill twice on a CD and you will be asked to play it back. You will then be asked to identify the fill from a set of three examples provided. The tempo is ♩=70.

Test 2: Groove Recall

The examiner will play you a two bar groove repeated on a CD twice. You will be asked to play back the groove as you have heard it on the CD. The examiner will then ask you to identify the style of the groove you have played from a list of three possibilities. A full list of potential styles is printed in the Syllabus Guide. The tempo is ♩=105.

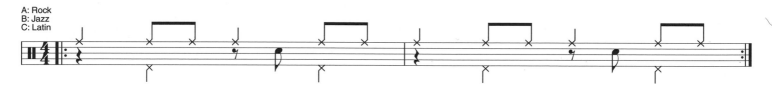

General Musicianship Questions

You will be asked five General Musicianship Questions at the end of the exam. The examiner will ask questions based on pieces you have played in the exam. Some of the theoretical topics can be found in the Technical Exercises.

Topics:

i)   Music theory
ii)   Knowledge of your instrument

The music theory questions will cover the recognition of the following at this grade:

> Any and all music signs as displayed on the stave

The instrument knowledge questions will cover the following topics at this grade:

> Names and position of all drum voices
> Procedures for tuning drums
> Procedures for changing a snare drum head
> Stylistic awareness of cymbal sounds as played in the pieces

Questions on all these topics will be based on pieces played by you in the exam. Tips on how to approach this part of the exam can be found in the Rockschool Companion Guide and on the Rockschool website: *www.rockschool.co.uk*.

The Guru's Guide To Drums Grade 5

This section contains some handy hints compiled by Rockschool's Drums Guru to help you get the most out of the performance pieces. Do feel free to adapt the tunes to suit your playing style. Remember, these tunes are your chance to show your musical imagination and personality.

The stickings shown in the music are suggestions only. Feel free to use different sticking combinations as they suit you. Please also note that any solos featured in the full mixes are not meant to be indicative of the standard required for the grade. The track listings below are grouped: 1-16: full mixes; 7-12: backing tracks without clicks; and 13-18: backing tracks with clicks.

Drums Grade 5 Tunes

Rockschool tunes help you play the hit tunes you enjoy. The pieces have been written by top pop and rock composers and players according to style specifications drawn up by Rockschool.

The tunes printed here fall into two categories. The first category can be called the 'contemporary mainstream' and features current styles in today's charts. The second category of pieces consists of 'roots styles', those classic grooves and genres which influence every generation of performers.

CD full mix track 1, backing tracks 7 & 13: Alka Setzer

This rock 'n' roll revival track in the style of the Stray Cats builds the drum part atmospherically from the beginning. The opening groove is played quietly with quarter note and off-beat eighth note kick drum beats and the hi hat played with the foot. The opening calls for brushes and you should look to develop the part in the cont. sim. sections. The break out section during the bass solo is counted with the hi hat foot and there are stabbed fills. The recording gives some ideas for the solo section based on rolls and other techniques. The groove in the guitar solo is played with sticks and is louder. Note the triplet hi hat groove in the final bars and watch for the characteristic fill at the end.

Composer: Simon Troup.

CD full mix track 2, backing tracks 8 & 14: Sidewinder

The opening drum groove in this Metallica style track is played medium. Note the bar of 3/4 at the end of each of the first three sets of four bars in this section and the fills. The groove in the main section is kick drum orientated (played in eighth notes) with alternating crash and ride cymbal patterns. The triplets are played around the kit. There is plenty of scope for you to develop the part and take advantage of the rhythmical variations in the second half.

Composer: Hussein Boon.

CD full mix track 3, backing tracks 9 & 15: All Funked Up

The groove in this funk track is mainly orthodox and features an off-beat eighth note kick drum beat with open hi hats on the first eighth note of each bar. There are stabbed fills. The secondary groove has a dotted eighth note and sixteenth note kick drum patterns and the cymbal switches to the ride; later this is developed to include drum voices played in unison. Note how the dynamics switch from soft to loud.

Composer: Jason Woolley.

CD full mix track 4, backing tracks 10 & 16: D & A

There is a high degree of variety in this Brit pop piece, starting with the ad libing on cymbals and toms before moving to the main groove played in eighth notes on snare and kick drum (note how the snare if off the beat here) and on open hi hat. This groove pattern is developed and features unison toms, kick and snare. There is further rhythmic variation during the harmonic section played on the guitar before a restatement of the main groove. Experiment with the part in the second half and think about how you would add expressive and dynamic contrasts to build more colour.

Composer: Noam Lederman.

CD full mix track 5, backing tracks 11 and 17: Bust Up

This modern punk pop piece is fun to play and features a wealth of variation in the part. The drum groove propels the song forward and is played at quite a lick. The eighth note tom-snare opening sets the pace and this then opens out into quite a spacious groove played mainly in quarter notes on snare and kick but with off-beat kick eighths for variation. Use the dynamics to build up to the unison passages with the other instruments (for example in bars 23-24) while the quick fills at the end of sections likewise build interest. The groove in the solo sections is more orthodox and is your chance to let rip.

Composers: Joe Bennett & Simon Troup.

CD full mix track 6, backing tracks 12 & 18: X-Blues III

A revival of an old Rockschool tune from 1993, this blues-shuffle groove is mainly orthodox in construction and is played in eighth notes on the kick and quarter notes on the snare with quarter note open hi hats. The development of the groove has eight to the bar on the snare which needs a light touch and dynamic variation not to sound heavy. There is much scope for development in the second half of the song during the bass and guitar solos.

Composer: Deirdre Cartwright.

CD Musicians:

Guitars: Keith Airey; Deirdre Cartwright; Hussein Boon
Bass: Henry Thomas
Drums: Noam Lederman; Peter Huntington
Keyboards and programming: Alastair Gavin

Drums Grade 5 Marking Schemes

The table below shows the marking scheme for the Drums Grade 5 exam.

ELEMENT	PASS	MERIT	DISTINCTION
Piece 1	13 out of 20	15 out of 20	17+ out of 20
Piece 2	13 out of 20	15 out of 20	17+ out of 20
Piece 3	13 out of 20	15 out of 20	17+ out of 20
Technical Exercises	11 out of 15	12–13 out of 15	14+ out of 15
Either Sight Reading *or* Improvisation & Interpretation	6 out of 10	7–8 out of 10	9+ out of 10
Ear Tests	6 out of 10	7–8 out of 10	9+ out of 10
General Musicianship Questions	3 out of 5	4 out of 5	5 out of 5
Total Marks	**Pass: 65%+**	**Merit: 75%+**	**Distinction: 85%+**

The table below shows the markings scheme for the Drums Grade 5 Performance Certificate and the Level 2 Band Exam.

ELEMENT	PASS	MERIT	DISTINCTION
Piece 1	14 out of 20	16 out of 20	18+ out of 20
Piece 2	14 out of 20	16 out of 20	18+ out of 20
Piece 3	14 out of 20	16 out of 20	18+ out of 20
Piece 4	14 out of 20	16 out of 20	18+ out of 20
Piece 5	14 out of 20	16 out of 20	18+ out of 20
Total Marks	**Pass: 70%+**	**Merit: 80%+**	**Distinction: 90%+**

Entering Rockschool Exams

Entering a Rockschool exam is easy. Please read through these instructions carefully before filling in the exam entry form. Information on current exam fees can be obtained from Rockschool by ringing 020 8332 6303 or by logging on to our website *www.rockschool.co.uk*.

• You should enter for your exam when you feel ready.

• You can enter for any one of three examination periods. These are shown below with their closing dates.

PERIOD	DURATION	CLOSING DATE
Period A	1st February to 15th March	1st December
Period B	1st May to 31st July	1st April
Period C	23rd October to 15th December	1st October

These dates will apply from 1st September 2006 until further notice

• Please complete the form giving the information required. Please fill in the type and level of exam, the instrument, along with the period and year. Finally, fill in the fee box with the appropriate amount. You can obtain up to date information on all Rockschool exam fees from the website: *www.rockschool.co.uk*. You should send this form with a cheque or postal order (payable to Rockschool Ltd) to the address shown on the order form. **Please also indicate on the form whether or not you would like to receive notification via email.**

• Applications received after the expiry of the closing date may be accepted subject to the payment of an additional fee.

• When you enter an exam you will receive from Rockschool an acknowledgement letter or email containing a copy of our exam regulations.

• Rockschool will allocate your entry to a centre and you will receive notification of the exam, showing a date, location and time as well as advice of what to bring to the centre. We endeavour to give you four weeks' notice of your exam.

• You should inform Rockschool of any cancellations or alterations to the schedule as soon as you can as it is usually not possible to transfer entries from one centre, or one period, to another without the payment of an additional fee.

• Please bring your music book and CD to the exam. You may not use photocopied music, nor the music used by someone else in another exam. The examiner will sign each book during each examination. You may be barred from taking an exam if you use someone else's music.

• You should aim to arrive for your Grade 5 exam fifteen minutes before the time stated on the schedule.

• Each Grade 5 exam is scheduled to last for 25 minutes. You can use a small proportion of this time to tune up and get ready.

• Two to three weeks after the exam you will receive a copy of the examiner's mark sheet. Every successful player will receive a Rockschool certificate of achievement.